Posting the Watch

To Myron Schreck —
with warm regards and
best wishes with your
work. I appreciate your
kindness.
                    [signature]
                    11/15/15

Posting the Watch

Poems by Michele F. Cooper

Turning Point

Published by Turning Point
P.O.Box 541106
Cincinnati, OH 45254-1106

ISBN: 9781933456850
LCCN: 2007936113

Poetry Editor: Kevin Walzer
Business Editor: Lori Jareo

Visit us on the web at www.turningpointbooks.com

for Ruth Whitman
and Herbert Woodward Martin
everlasting thanks

The following journals published poems from this collection:

"A Cup of Daily Gruel," "When the Storms Die," and "Snake Eyes," in *Kalliope* (2007)

"Baby Reds" and "Sadie's Eye Turns In at the Fleeting Thought of Spring," in *Terra Incognita* (2006)

"Ray of Hope" and "Rounding the Pass," in *Southern Hum* (2005)

"Rounding the Narrow Pass," in *Paumonok Review* (2001)

"You Left Your Horse Behind," "Snake-Eyes," "Sun-Ups and Night Chills," "How the Fences Crumble," "Sadie Larkin Posting the Watch," and "Sadie, Glad Warrior," as a group, won Honorable Mention in the *Literally Horses* Poetry Contest (2001)

"Sadie Remembers Her Marbles...," in *Poetry Motel* (2000) "Going Down to Zero," "Main Street and Wrinkly Wools," "Three Parts Fertilizer, One Part Sun," "Sadie Looks to the Trees," and "Sadie Larkin Posting the Watch," in *Online Poetry & Story* (1999)

"In Autumn the Yellows Are Brilliant," in *CQ (California Quarterly)* (1998)

"An Open Palm Means Welcome" and "Blackbirds," in *Kyosaku* (1998)

"Boulder Creek," in *RI Women Speak* (National Museum of Women in the Arts) (1997)

"Hey, You Left Your Horse Behind," in *Stable Companion* (1996)

"How the Skin Burns Red," in *Nedge* (the Poetry Mission) (1996)

"Bird of Youth" as "Sweet Bird of Youth," in *Black Buzzard Review* (1996)

"Tomato Harvest," in *Faultline* (1995)

"Four Thoughts on Being Tidy and Mighty Fine" and "Her Daily Gruel," in *Appropospourri* (1995)

"Kentucky Bluegrass Blues," in *Atom Mind* (1995)

"Taking the Snake-Path Every Damn Night," in *Arachne* (1994)

"Sadie Does a Little Jig on the Long Road Home," in an earlier version entitled "Hey, Man, Where's My Lines?" in *World Order* (1987-88)

"Blue Flames and Skeeter Blues," "Sadie Larkin Posting the Watch," and "Dark of the Moon," in *Women on Women* (chapbook) (1986)

"Dark of the Moon," as "Blues for a Beige Quarter-Moon," in *Sea-Change* (1985)

Friends, relatives, poets, listeners and readers helped a great deal with their support for this collection, but special thanks are gratefully offered to Herbert Woodward Martin, Janet Kaplan, Barbara Schweitzer, Pat

Hegnauer, and Kathryn Kulpa, outstanding writers, for their expert counsel. The Virginia Center for the Creative Arts and Vermont Studio Center offered time and space to work on this book.

Table of Contents

High Hills

River Valley

Four Thoughts on Being Tidy and Mighty Fine

Sadie Larkin, blood racing down her arms and legs,
        forehead flushed from the heat,
        the knitted brows, the whispers.
She is talking to herself,
        telling herself how the signs
        mean little or nothing,
they can't count everything,
        can't know it all.
Damn them, she cries.
Damn the signs that cross Sadie Larkin,
        shake her pride.

She is walking down the west field,
        sun dropping fast,
gnats raising hell with the herds,
old crow flying south
        under the honking geese.
Go on and duck, you bloody son.
You the smart one, ducking,
        taking the low path,
        you the clever one!

Curse the field-rock, too, she's hollering.
Been pulling stones here fifteen years
        if it's a day.
Had this hill cleaned right and proper
        a couple years back.
Now it's full of rock!
Break the goddamn tractor for sure—
        break Bessie's poor leg
        —break stride.

It is a long walk past the west field,
stalks leaning on their last legs,
        dry and tired, tired and dry,
        witches with wrinkles in cold firelight.

Pull 'em up, damnation,
        pull out the rot, clean it up.
Let the ground breathe deep for once.
Goddamn earth is suffocating!

Hide-Out Dry as Dust

She pokes her nose into the shadow places
>   tucked between the barn and the back-house.
Hardly a place for seeds to find some dirt,
>   you'd think, if you did think on these things.
No way the sun can angle in,
>   spring breezes, April showers.

It's dry as dust in here, she looks from weed to weed.
Body can hardly find herself some air,
>   *never mind a place to sit alone.*

The purples and yellows surprise her,
>   four feet tall on twiggy stems.
Stalks come through the metal scraps,
>   pay no mind to railroad ties.
Even at that they're leaning back some,
>   bending out of harm's way,
backing past the dead rose,
>   looking for heaven.

Everything's paper thin but the thorns,
>   she's said this before.
Ain't that always the way.

Why'd you come out here, Sadie?
>   Sitting rock too exposed?
Del still working in the barn,
>   Pa in the house,
>   Ma in the stony ground?

Taking the Snake-Path Every Damn Night

Way down the valley,
    she sees the row cottages,
        curls of smoke winding out
        from tin chimneys,
    work pants upside down on the line,
kitchen gardens muddy from Tuesday's rain.

They're always home, she murmurs
    in her white breath,
        doing their fires and too much cooking,
        keeping their little piece of dirt
    tended for the neighbors and the reverend.
Damned if they ain't tidy, and mighty fine.

Why do I take this snake-path every night?
    she wonders,
        chewing the words like cud.
        Getting lazy, I reckon,
  plumb tired, too.
Working with my feet instead of my head.

Sadie's Eye Turns In at the Fleeting Thought of Spring

Spring is a passing fine idea,
fleeced with colts and lambikins
winking at you and your
wet, steaming nostrils,
pressing out the wrinkles
on a wildflower meadow,

then folding in on itself.

Main Street and Wrinkly Wools

Sadie Larkin in the cobbled square
smoothing her wrinkly wools,
feeling sere and dusty
near the lace-necked ladies
and their flannel babies,
everything in place,
everything right and ready
        on the waterside marigold path.

No one yells at Wickerton Falls.
We got a nice little town here,
and hey,—smiling—leaning back—
        we like it fine that way.

Look at our lovely swans,
they jump a pause to tell you.
Couples stick together,
        marry for life, don't you know.

Throw some bits of bread
to the quacky mallards
there by the paddleboats.
How come the boys are so much
        prettier'n the ladies?

Yes, ma'am, we like the preening swans
gliding by our new fall tweeds,
gobbling our moldy muffins,
cutting narrow water-trails,
gaggling their way upstream.
        Everything's right in Wickerton Falls.

I need air, she mutters,
—need my mare.
Too hard breathing
on this little bank.
I need a big, long trail.
Need some time.
              O, I need time.

A Couple of Heavy Notes on Being Accountable

She is trying to hold her strength, . . .
    house-chores keeping her under wraps
    while the sun spins a finch-yellow light
    gallivanting through the sheepskins.

It's the hardest row to hoe,
    . . . my lady.

Nothing much proceeding
    on Slipper Hill
    since the barn burned to cinders
    and Clay, her beau, sold the herd.

Crickets scratching out a living
    in the noisy August shade,
    and she could easily grab
    Ma's favorite quilt
    and raise a mountain of z's
    in no time!

Take her no time or less
    to skip the hoeing and chopping
    and mopping and washing
    and tying and milking
    and drying and packing.

Another summer Tuesday
    squeezing into gear,
    high noon marking the hour
    while the sun tramps west.

Reading the Furrowed Brow

Sad Selina yanking her chain,
barking thunder from a troubled gut
out back beneath the steps,

    big storm rising from the belly-bottom,
    some folks wishing
    she'd quiet down already.

        How come Sadie can read the signs,
        hear the fierce hunger in the furious bark,
        the strain to dash across the road,

            nuzzle a hand, find a friend,
            and nothing shows on the great doggie face
            except the watering eyes, the knitted brow?

Kentucky Bluegrass Blues

Sadie Larkin, poised in the window after wild
storms, fingernails tapping code on the counter-
boards, mind racing with last night's wind,
wondering how the rain can stop so sudden, how the
change comes, how come the gray mare took off
again, it's four times, count 'em, and the barn's real
empty under that leaky shingle roof.

You in trouble, Sadie? Heard the rain and
knew you were in for it? Well, you saw
them leaks. Saw them, felt them, touched
the seams. No way you couldn't know the
place wasn't sealed up tight. Too old, Sadie,
not enough upkeep. Never mind the barn
being biggest in the county, big and brown
against the glen. Never guess *that* place
leaks,—*no,* sir.

What next? she asks the hedge-rows, big storm-tears
drenching the tall grass. *Drops fall so heavy you can hear
them soaking the earth, soaking it good, putting out the sun
three days for starters.*

I don't get you, gal. Your daddy taught you
how to mend wall, how to look straight on
the wet stains, check the soft spots, follow
the water-trails right to the dripping places.
He never took his eyes off the big sores,
never ducked by. Why can't you look out
like him, Sadie? You blind?

Damn the rain, she cries. *Damn the rain! Damn the mare! Damn the leaks! I can't shingle that roof. Can't move the damn ladder, haven't got the tools right, haven't had a soul here, it's years already, giving me a hand with this place. No fair, Daddy! No fair you running off, leaving me to shoulder everything myself. And where's my damn mare? I need that mare more'n I need my supper. Got a bad feeling, too, feeling this time she's never coming back. Not that anybody'd want her. Used old thing! Gray-haired, limping, whinnying, stamping, hungry, stubborn old thing! You come back here so's I can get on with the days and nights! You hear?!*

Baby Reds

The root is long
and hungry lean,
tapers into the
black earth
under
scratchy,
browning
leaves.

Scruffy
root-hairs
reach
blindly
for worms
and water,
reach around
the tiny
purple
potatoes

that clutch
their parsnip
mother
for all
her anemic
strength,
and

very

slowly

swell.

How the Skin Burns Red

She cowers under the porch roof, watches the trees bend
        to strain in the roaring gusts.
The sleet is hard, acid in the icy stones as they graze
        her hands, bounce off the steps.

      Warily she soaks up the hisses and whirs,
      dances in place,
      waits her turn to dash for cover,
      count the possibilities.

      But the whistle hissing has gotten to her,
      and the numbing fingers
      cannot find the pocket-slits
      in the torn, tweed fabric of things.

An Open Palm Means Welcome

She shows an open eye, hopes
the open palm will reach her, wrap
around her arm, pull her off

    a steep and rocky cliff.

The sky goes cloudy gray.
Birds race for cover, branches
press for space, the kid up-road

    bleats hard for its absent ma.

In the sky, a thunderhead. The palm
reaches out, makes a word curl
in the air, pulls around, then pulls back.

    Heads up, Sadie,
    eyes to the granite rock.

Blackbirds

Two black birds
riding the mountain winds,
looking for prey,
for the old cave door,

closed now
by last year's fall.

Her Mother's Recipe

The stew-pot holds a confection
    of peppers and onions,
    chunks of fatty beef.

Brown juice leaves a pasty trail
    on the old spice tins,
    white pepper, paprika.

The salt taste on her swollen thumb
    unnerves her with its eloquence,
    annihilates the old flat crust.

She will pick out the soured celeries,
    cut the soft tomatoes into
    hundreds of tiny pieces,
    curse the missing pot cover,
    reach for the flowered soup-bowl.

But the wooden spoon has broken
    at the burn-spot,
    there isn't a crust in the house,
    and the stove won't clean.

It's been a long afternoon
    of headaches and heaving.

Mother's recipe isn't working.

Blue Flames, Skeeter Blues

Long white squash boiling heavy on Sadie's coal-stove, white steam sweeting the fruits over the burner, tendering them, the slight, fragrant swell enticing the flesh to a succulence it couldn't know before.

You can taste it, can't you, Sadie? All cooked to a turn and ready for serving? Can't you taste it 'fore it passes your mouth? You take a whiff of the past, put out a smile of knowing, and feel the spit come up like the temperature down the back-end of July. You're a cool one, Sadie Larkin, tasting things when they're not on your plate yet. Who taught you to do that, girl? Who was it?

How to eat this meal? she considers. *Shall I pierce the flesh with a silver fork? Lift it over the steaming heat? See if it holds its shape? See if the flesh splits where the prongs cut into the dark green skin and the steamy sweat oozes into the cooler air and down the curving flanks? How shall I serve it up?*

You never been a true eater, Sadie, told you that many a time. But you do cook good. And you know your fruits. I seen you pickin' up them squashes out the garden—passing by the overgrowns, checking out the babies, and going for the middlins, just right, tasty and firm, real tasty every time. 'Bout as much to picking as growing, I'd say. I know about that. I ain't dumb.

I am boiling in the cauldron. The spears are in my sides and chest. And I am watching the pale red, clear white juices spill

*out. They run down my face and thighs, painful shy of the blue
flames below, in an avalanche of salt white pulp, afraid of the
raw and sour aftertaste that sometimes comes without calling.*

Coward, I call you, Sadie. You plant 'em and pick
'em, but ain't eating the whole meal's how I see it.
You want the insides, but damn the stems. And
what're you peeling the skin off for? You think the
skin don't go down OK? It's thin, Sadie, soft and
tender. And it won't turn your stomach no-ways.
Never mind them beetles and skeeter markings. You
check the skins—both sides—with a nice easy touch.
And watch out the boiling water, for god's sake!

Sadie Imagines Unloading the Gear from Her Broad, Unpadded Shoulders

Bringing yesterday's baggage into the light,
holding it up for all to see,
parading the dents down Main Street,
through the aisles of the general store,
walkway in front of the diner, the tailor shop,
looking to see who catches the leathery sheen,
who picks up on the throbbing load
booming like a big bass drum
down the music-hall.

You'd think the pack was dripping
with sludge, by god,
clots darkening the stream-bed,
curling the edges,
bright rust flagging folks,
slipping out the cracks
and thickening the broth
before it all goes bad.

Going Down to Zero

At 20 degrees the bleating begins,
short notes, separate and sorrowing.
At 10, it's a long harangue.
The legs are frozen leather and
bones of ice,
the ears are gone,
and breathing hurts the tongue.

Where is the resting-place?

You stand at the window,
listen to the distant bleats,
wonder, won't they ever hear it,
ever feel that depth of cold,
that searing of soul,
that dying of Ma again and again
and again?

Dark of the Moon

Sadie Larkin, breast high, climbing astride her great brown mare, pinholes of light shining in the centers of her eyes, stars blinking back, the breath-mist.

It is evening, just now evening. The atmosphere is full with deep pink and dense gray, so thick she cannot see beyond the scallions and peppers she is dicing for dinner. She feels as though she is outside in the coming dusk, bathed in mauve, not in the wood kitchen, chopping.

She would ride that mare, Sadie Larkin, but the beast won't move, won't take her into the night, careening along the country roads under the bright quarter-moon. She's a stuck mare, Sadie; stop kicking the flanks; stop shouting.

Later, when the sky is almost navy in the east, the thick air spreads out some; and though she feels like a walk on the old hill road, she folds the laundry carefully enough, humming a country tune that caught the top of her mind. She is folding, humming, folding and humming—dreaming early scenes in double exposure.

Sadie Larkin, poised on the great horse, urging her on beyond the paddock gate, watching her snuff in the far air, nostrils quivering with heat and cold, wanting to fly, but held.

In the dark ebony night, a few stars peek through the cotton clouds, nothing like the great quarter-moon reflecting light like a fragment of evening sun, blazing in its way, enlightening the clouds, pouring

over the birch leaves just beyond her view. The
fence-roses are failing in the choppy air. Rose-
o'-Sharons past the picket fence are pink and alive in
the cold light. She turns off the lamp on her desk,
where she is reading of dragons and nightmare
horse-mothers, and hums old tunes in the darkness,
moonlight all around the house like cold heat,
hugging her to herself in an orange burlap chair.

*Get moving, Sadie Larkin, it's a long life but the night is
short. Best find the way to charge the mare, quicken her,
before the moon goes down and she lays off whinnying for the
open road. What is wrong with your horse, Sadie Larkin?
Why won't she take you?*

At 2:20 she has rehearsed the necessary
conversations, puzzled out a few small answers,
realized that emptiness is not a lost path. If only, if
only . . . she almost thinks, putting the cat out with a
nuzzle and a silent I'm sorry; if only . . . It is a long
muse as the toothbrush goes back and forth, back
and forth, and she has to smile, as she wipes the sink
for yet another time, at how the sublime and the
ridiculous so often strike a match and make it
together in the dark of night, under cover.

Rolling Plains

Looking for the Pendulum to Mark
a New Day

There's a time for everything,—
        that's what they say,—
and this particular hour ain't it.

Real clock-time, I'm talking about—
        big clock-time—
time to fly across the high hills,
        sweet mare sweating by me,
time to flap my wings so fast
        there's a gray-white blur
when the wind catches the rise,
        time even for a nap,
go walk the riverbank,
        double back for tea,
time cooking the soups and hashes,
        country radio twanging,
plenty of nuzzling the nutmeg man.

Or, honey, there's no time for anything—
        and that's my tired old song.
Been singing that song since I was
        knee-high to a cornflower.
You *know* that. I *know* you know.

And then Aunt Sal comes by in a real stew,
        so hot and tired she can hardly talk.
Wants to be let alone, Sade.
Just everybody go away
        and leave me alone,
she's mean and grumbling.
Lemme be,

lemme just do my work.
Give me a chance to catch my breath.

I know that song backwards and front,
      hear?
Has to do with sweet naps,
and that's the juicy part of it—
        two o'clock snooze,
        catnap in the rocker,
        half an hour after supper,
when you *can* doze off
in a honey's sweet arms.
      Mmmm.

Hey, Wait - Just - A - Minute!
Don't talk to me about naps
       when there's all day to go
       and no way to duck it!

Rounding the Pass 1

She slips into the woods between the scrub-oaks and
the Big Daddy Pine. It's the first time, and she wags
her head, looking up at the pass she never knew was
set just there and more in reach than ever she'd
guessed.

Damned it if ain't space for two, let alone one, she says,
wondering why, why, why she never passed that way
before. She's been looking down at that Big Daddy
Pine twenty, thirty years, if it's a day. Been hearing
about that hidden pass since she was a bean sprout,
how the bears come down from the mountain and
push their black bear way through the trees, running
to escape the blaze that chased them one and all with
its curling tongues. Pushed right through, don't you
know, and made a path no more seen since *who* can
remember.

She heard tell about it, though. Heard tell witches
and coyotes scream bloody murder the whole night
long if anyone's down that way past sundown. Heard
tell three boys from the next county went on
anyways and never came out. That's right. Their
daddies and the sheriffs combed the place for twelve
days after, and nothing came out excepting some
mighty haggard old men with bee stings, sweat, and
skeeter bites up and down their dog-tired arms.

After that, neither Sadie nor pretty much anyone else
been down that side of the creek, though Sadie, of
course, she's prowled nearby plenty of times, and
one cloudy afternoon, after chores, feeling a strange

sorrow for no particular reason and some of that red hot anger she knew too well, she moseys down in that direction, thinking she can find some early berries before the deer get 'em all—maybe see that baby bear everyone's talking about.

Down she goes, tasting berries and bark on her dry tongue, all the time wondering about searching out the closed pass, wondering if she'll find her way in again, wondering if she'll have the vinegar to try cutting through. Hell, she's cut through near about everything else by now, what with the fire and Pa killing the mare, Clay turning away that once— ending up alone on the farm. You can't pass through any more'n those dark nights. She's been thinking about these things too much lately anyhow. She knows that. She doesn't need big brother Del or worrying Clay telling her to throw it aside.

She puts a knife into the basket, wraps a kerchief around her neck, and starts out under the straw cover of her walking-hat. *Good, good land*, she thinks, looking back at the farm when she catches the first rise. Ridges look like shoulders, rocks like bones. *It's making it here's the thing*, she thinks, *not but that the place isn't right. The place is definitely right.* She understands that about the hills and fields—feels it in the back of her eyes where thinking starts. *Even pretty in a scruffy kind of way. It's not the place. It's the work's what it is— yes, sir. Enough damn work for a full-time pair of hands, two mules, and then it'd be hard finding a day off.*

Going down the creek is practically sassy today what with the first corn ready to bring in.

Hell, she says, *it'll have to wait.*

Rummaging around the creek bed, Sadie finds flint
and some strange pink pebbles—not a mushroom or
berry in sight, and the trees a solid fence. *Nothing can
get in there*, she says, making turn after turn after turn
as the river winds its way around the rocks and
knobby crests of water reeds and grasses. Pricker
bushes so thick and high, you need a locomotive for
protection, thorn tips looking straight at you, waiting
to push right through your heavy skirts, cut your
legs, rip your knuckles, and you trying to save the
skin on your one working arm,—it doesn't take a
coward to squeak some and turn tail. Anyone would.

Today, though, she is running an adventure, hair
down her back, flowing free without the kerchief as
she moves toward the creek falls. She takes long
strides, but not fast. She is thinking as she goes,
letting it set about Clay coming by the other Sunday,
trying to talk nice and set up a time.

I don't want it, she says aloud. *I wish I did, but I don't.*

She walks harder and her hair rides the wind like a
mane. She'll go down by the grove of pines, see what
she can see. Grab her basket, tuck her skirts, and
push on in.

Don't let it slip, Sadie. Don't go limp!

Three Parts Fertilizer, One Part Sun

The vine climbs slowly
toward the kitchen door
from the dim north hall,
barely a chance of making it work,
    but trying—trying
        to work a destiny—
            not even a whisper of curling up
                and browning out the dream!

Daring ivy, deep in gloom,
putting out her flaccid leaves,
weakening from the search for sun,
dry around the edges,
new leaves getting smaller and smaller
    as they bravely push forth
        their wondering baby lives.

What is this endless travail to get born,
get up and on the road?
    Can you call the question, Sadie?
        Can you beat it into the light?

How the Fences Crumble

Filly waits in the grassy field,
      prances to the fence
      when she's whistled at,
      studies the sugar,
      eyeing it, head cocked,
      tasting it, forbidden there
      in the large bronze hand.

She's heard about the cubes of snow,
      heard they make you wild
      with delight,
      make you leap and prance,
      forget the better business
      of pastures and grasses.

You see that piece of sweet promise—
      almost makes you plumb forget yourself—
      go on over the hill
      and never look back.

Sadie's Holiday Comes and Goes with Due Thought

Go keep the holiday to yourself,
Sadie Larkin,
no one at the dinner table,
no one walking the sunshine,
no talk.

You had your chances—
you know right well:
hot casserole over Town Hall,
cold brunch with Gossip Sal,
buffet roast at Nana Hart's.

But you picked Hepzibah, honey,
black cat O'Reilly,
twangy tunes on the ray-dee-o,
baking and straightening
and thinking through folks' ways.

You could've seen the hermit, too,
don't forget that charity thought.
You passed it by, and I see it
like a low moon crossing the woods.
Sure enough, the hours done passed,

the whole countryside doing their dishes
right in time with Sadie Larkin,
everyone planning on new days, too,
maybe make some family time
with one sweet wood-stove love,

maybe hang the laundry out the line,
maybe let it *all* come out the cracks.

Sadie Remembers Her Marbles, Goes Back to the Place Where She Last Saw Them, and—O My—They're Still There—Right Where She Left Them!

Hold back the hearty soups,
the spicy cinnamon pies.
You're giving it all away till your bowl's
gone empty, a basket of husks
on the back steps,
old stalks, empty gourds.

Best now, finish your plate,
savor the turnip smell,
and pick up your shawl—
dragging on the ground like that!

Wipe it down with a piece of cloth,
spread it on the porch to dry,
away from the blazing sun.

Remember those stitches—
you hooked them round yourself?

And now they sit in the mud
while you pack the quart jars?
throw in an extra bread?

No, Sadie!
No, I say!

She Left Her Horse Behind

He idles by the fence, I tell you. Waiting.
    Nibbling green and yellow grasses
    in a dry meadow under the dew,
    trying to keep his eyes down,
    staring at the meadow-ground,
    taking up the limp greens,
    wondering where the taste went,
    wondering, was there ever
    really summer after all?

In the dank morning light,
    the cold curls under the brown horse-hairs.
    The barn felt good, he thought,
    as they nudged him out the double doors,
    sweeter than it has in days,
    almost good enough to linger in,
    lay back, hold to,
    not set about the chill November air.
    Better watch that, he whinnied.
    Stay here too long,
    damn barn starts looking better'n
    the crisp outdoors.

So he clip-clopped out, I watched it,
    and it *was* too cold.
    Dew all over the ground
    barely sparkling at the end of the dark,
    cold coming right on
    through the silver shoes,
    themselves hurting bad, it's a week now.

Can't stay out here, he needled himself.

No blanket. No clover.
No wild rides in the hills and valley-passes.
Can't stay in this field, always looking down,
always nibbling, head-shaking,
pretending nothing else worth doing.

Can't go in neither.
    Too hot the stilly spaces.
    Too stale when morning stokes
    and others foul the air.
    Can't breathe in there.
    Can't move out here.
    Enough to make you shake and shudder,
    think about not-breathing,
    passing on the limp straw,
    passing it all.

That's what he thinks, I'm telling you.
Heard him muttering just around sun-up.

Sadie Looks for the Moon on a Moonless Night

Black water splashes
the rocky riverbanks,
rushes round her ankles
and the slippery grasses,
grabs at sunsets
and summer scents,
drapes her in garlands
of white petals iced
by cold stars,
warmed by tireless
lapping gusts.

Who says the lights are out
in this windswept
watermelon night?

A Cup of Daily Gruel

She can hear the hungry grunting,
nervous pig-feet knocking the wood floor
long before she passes the porch—
      pig slops sliding around the rusty pail.

Rancid brew makes your head turn,
pigs snorting like wild boars
      getting the first whiffs.
Melon rind's the worst by far,
      maybe squashes, yellow and green.
Even in the cool September rain
      they're like to send you reeling.

If it weren't for the stench,
she could probably stand the whole thing better.

Why am I laboring anyways?
      I'm asking.
I can quit this farm
      anytime I take a mind to—
pack the handle-case Del left behind,
      lay in a couple of skirts,
      the brown knit blouse,
      Mama's fine shoes,
      her best string of pearls.
That's right—sure! . . . I can pack them pearls,
      pretty ballies, all of 'em twins
      shining pink and blue in the bedroom light.

I might even wear *them pearls some day!*

When the Storms Die

Slow oil leaks through the granite wall,
fixing Sadie's heavy glare.
Cracks change from brown to black—
then melt to widening stains.

Yellow lights go dark in warehouse yards.

Sadie canters backwards
for a last, teetering glance.
She hears a scream in the growing dusk,
one low whistle,
an expiration of breath—
then it's still as a hurricane's eye.
She can hear her rapid breathing,
claps of thunder in the open air,
one cricket singing her broken song.

What are you doing here, Sadie?
After Pa's nighttime howling and
Del's Thanksgiving temper—
haven't you heard enough?

Turn! and run!!
(I'm rolling out the gate!)
Pull up hard on the reins
and back-track to the barn—
where the oil's in the tractor,
screams come in nightmares,
and the still air smells of peppermint
when the storms die.

In Autumn the Yellows Are Brilliant

Lightning tree hugs the windy road
bracing the old stone fence, upright
while the bark peels, upright
while the scrub bushes beneath
her arms wither, upright
as a stance against the groaning
wood, the creaking, the unpruned
rays of hope upturned, up right.

Sadie Looks to the Trees Past
the Orchard and Considers the Wind
in Her Wings

Brown hawk whips across the field
    in her black feather hat,
flattens the yellow grass
    when her swoop is low,
whips round the ancient trunk
    in centrifugal grace.

Sadie watches her dip and swerve,
    fearlessly choosing her fit path,
thinks of trading places for a spell,
    taking her turn to bore through the air,
great Sadie wings outspread,
    making her mark on the grass—
        then lifting into the wind,
            flying to a distant skyline—
                if and when she has a mind to.

Boulder Creek

She never looks back—sure it's best that way—keeps
the focus on the here and now, where she's got to be
—*got* to. She peers down the green canyon, old forest
strangely still around her and the mare, trees covered
in dusty summer, talking some when the wind blows,
cracking a branch now and again, then settling back
with bird-calls and day-crickets. She likes looking
ahead these days, up the steep hills, checking for
trails under the crackling leaves, wondering if the
markers are still there, if anything's left whole.

What's behind is behind, she murmurs. No point
rehearsing it again. Even if the creek starts going the
wrong way, for god's sake, let it flow, set its little
pools, lap the raggedy shore under the leaves, catch
some sun the damn few times the rays cut past the
branches.

She gets up the hills in her own time, too, even when
the crags rise straight and the notches all filled with
slippery leaves.

Trees falling all along the path, sometimes coming
down without the roots turning up to keep them
company. Just the great trunks lying on the ground,
no hints of fungus or lightning or fire or wear-out.
What sends them down? She can hardly put words
on the question, wondering how to scale the
boulders where Clay pulled his fit that year she talked
of giving up and selling the place.

***

56

You never been a damned coward! he yelled. *And you never let on you'd leave!*

I'm not exactly leaving, Clay. I just can't keep it going by myself.

I'll help you more, he offered.

You already help as much as you want, Clay. And it doesn't feel good losing time at your own place. You got a lot of your own to do already.

I do what I choose, Sade.

That's for sure. But I need somebody full time. Used to be me, Pa, and Del couldn't even do it all. Then you coming over here and there, stealing time from your own crops to mow my hay, help me paint and patch the roof. It's hopeless, though, me trying to do seven things, every one taking more'n a body's got. I'm getting on, too, you can see that. Getting plumb fed up now and again. Wondering about getting it simpler. You know. We talked it over more than once-t.

I can't move in, Sade. The farm'd go to pieces if I left, and the kids'll have nothing after it's gone.

I know, Clay.

I got to think of them, Sade.

I know, Clay.

But I'm torn, too.

Sure.

And you're not.

No, I'm not. It's too much, weighing me down. I gotta make a change.

Don't box me, Sadie.

I'm not asking you for anything, Clay. Haven't done that in so long I can't remember the last time, what I even needed you for, whenever that was.

You make it sound like I don't care.

She looked up the crown ridge, knowing she should be looking right at him, telling him outright, *No, Clay, you don't care, really, not enough, anyways. And it's practically worse than not damn caring at all.* But she let him explain, nodding and mm-hmming so it seemed she was letting him right on off'n the hook, saying sure, she'd go home and think about all he'd said, and maybe, maybe there'd be a way to hang on a little longer. Maybe work something out somehow.

But why? Why would she?

***

She takes a sharp right turn off the wooded path, a sudden move, nothing the mare ever guessed. She herself hardly knows what she's about. The ground is strewn with broken limbs, trunks, years of leaves mulching the buried earth.

Getting into the shade makes her skin purse. Her eyes take in a pitch-black bird with a swath of white on fluttery wings.

Fly off while you can, pretty thing! she hollers, holding her place. *Don't wait!*

Snake-Eyes

Sadie clambers down the riverbed,
      half asleep in her heavy skirts
and looking for golden pebbles in the lapping water,
      scanning the ripples from high in the saddle.
Puffy cloud formations
      coil messages overhead.
Gray garters half-sleeping on the flat-rocks,
      single eyes moving to take her in.

This is not the first noon
      the pace is so lazy.
Cottonwoods watch the scene
      from their muddy banks.
They know the score.
If she keeps on like this,
      she'll never make it where she's going.
You can tell by the slow measured steps,
      the downward tilt
      of the hardened jaw,
how sorely bad the bad can be.

Why do you tarry on this
      April day, O Sadie?
What's ahead not to see?
      Why can't you meet it at the crossroad?

The mare is plumbed out under her weight.
She knows this walk outside and in:
      steady pace across the valley floor,
slow passing the forest hills,
      snail's pace down by the water.

She would rather gallop,
        I'm telling you.
Take off! See it if you can!
        Nose into the wind,
        eyes straight ahead,
        silk tail flicking the past aside.

High Hills

Bird of Youth

New road comes around
when the trees take to falling,
a wagon's-width spread
among the forest trunks,
curling out of sight

like a green and purple rain-bird.

Posting the Watch

Looking out for colts on the high north road,
needing the fresh warm wind to spread some sense
    on the raggedy fields,
set some right and proper paths
    through the winter woods,
straighten out the salt-sour smells
    curling up the valley,
break down for certain
    some of them hard-knock days and nights.

You are one crazy girl, Sadie.
Ain't nothing gonna put things right like that.

Don't see no colt breaking up-road, she granted,
    but aw hell, he'll come, sure as springtime.
    —always does,
excepting that one time back in summer . . .
    colt took off, by god, and stayed off, didn't he?
I keep seeing the going . . . weeks on end . . .
    deep down my mind's back eye.
Never figured that one out,
    probably never will.
Even said I didn't *care* that once't.
My, my . . . said I didn't care.

Sadie, you are one sorry number.
Can't even believe you hardly.

Best keep the watch anyways, I say.
Go on down the line, step finely,
    keep it going, *how*-ever.

You get to stopping now, get dry and start forgetting,
        hell — you'll plumb die,
            cracked and curled like an autumn leaf,
and that won't do, now or never, *no,* ma'am.
They will be no dying, I can tell you that.
No fun there, young *or* old.
        Can't bank it neither.

Tomato Harvest

one day shy of the full moon
and a surprise September frost

The basket is woven of wet and matted reeds
      gnarled into their holding form,
plump tomatoes bursting their
      soft red skins,
here and there a razor break
      showing the swollen flesh
two shades lighter in the slanting sun.

He is holding the basket with whitened hands,
      squeezing the handles into his skin.
The strings print patterns across the palms,
      ridges of pain when the blood flows back.

Why does he pace like a listening sparrow?
Is he worrying the fruits like raw eggs?
Is this his harvest worry-dance?

She adds armfuls of tomatoes to his growing load,
      hundreds of beefsteaks,
thousands and thousands of cherries,
      seven dozens of pickling greens.
She brings more and more to the basket,
      filling it past the rim
      and up to a shiny pyramid.

He lowers his arms, rippling with the weight.
He wants to stop her, saying,
It's too much, you're going too far,
      weighing me down.

The basket will come apart.
No, *no!* she stamps.
The basket is of wet and matted reeds,
    gnarled into their holding form.
It will never fall apart. Mark me!

Sadie Does a Little Jig on the Long Road Home

She is walking down this two-lane,
   see?
And stepping fine along
   those double yellow lines.
Two-stepping, you might call it,
   side-stepping,
doing her little jig,
   trying to get where she's going,
moving 'round, but *getting* there,
   if you get me.

And she's singing, hear?
   Singing blues—the darkest blue.
You can do that,
   sure,
sing your heart out
   like there's no tomorrow,
not for you, anyways, not when
   you so down in the heels
you can't see your eyelids
   through the salt water-fall.

You can sing 'em *high*,
   she says,
send those low-down blues
   high as a kite,
high as the clouds up there,
   those big white ice-cream clouds
over the back hills,
   the far hills, back a bit,
not those wispy spider webs

70

just overhead.

You see those ice-cream clouds,
                hear those blues,
and sing your eyes out
                till you get those babies
                up where they belong,
carrying your weighed-down baggage—
                all thousand pounds of it—
into a big, bountiful,
                flying aeroplane.

Not a real plane, mind,
                just a head-thought,
getting your sorrows into high gear,
                singing them out,
your big baggage blues,
                singing them
till you're gliding high,
                up where you wanted to be,
wanted to be always,
                always knew it, needed it,
wanted to be there all the days—
                night-times, day-times—
night-times, too.

Sure, she wants those
                night-times, too.
Get on off'n this low-down runway
                and out the door.
Real far.
        Real high.
                Real fast.

Clay's Song

Sadie Larkin, long hair limp from the damp night air,
walking the hard, packed ground over the hayfield.

It is midnight or beyond. The frogs are singing, but
she can't seem to hear them.

Sadie, Sadie, Sadie, it's me . . . Clay. I am watching
you cross the field and it's hard to believe! Your back
is straight, your head is high. By rights, you should
be dead this night.

Hey, Sadie, your skirts are dragging. You know your
brown skirts are still too long? Dragging over the
tamped earth, brushing the weeds along the path,
picking off pieces of twigs and dried leaves? You
know that? Can you hear the twigs breaking, swish
of the wool on your underskirt, little tug when the
skirt gets caught on a burr and won't let go till you
walk another step? Are you there, Sadie? Can you
hear me?

I was by the window, you know, back at the barn. I
seen your Pa kill the mare, though no one saw me
seeing. It wasn't a pretty scene. I felt like heaving,
seeing him beat her up like that. He was out of his
head, doing it so wild. Must have been crazy with
the axe and a pitchfork. Too much to take, that
about losing the girl and the new pastures in two
months' time. What kind of man can take it? Not
me, I know for sure . . . not me.

Still, the way that horse was crying, tore your heart

72

out. And I know you was close to her—too close, maybe. Maybe you was just too close to that big old horse. Riding out nights like you did, flying over the hills, riding like all get-out, like there been a fire down your heels. Where'd you go all those nights out? Everyone round here wants to know. It's not just your Pa. And him, of course, he'd have a natural interest. Me? I was just worried for you. Not prying, no, I wouldn't pry. Just worried, and maybe a little curious, sure.

Can't get far now, can you, though? Can't go flying out past the flats without a goddamn horse! So . . . how you gonna do it, gal?

Probably wondering that very thing right now— aren't you wondering?

Me? I had a horse once. Damn fine, too—gelding, with a white diamond on his nose, near about perfect. Me and that horse got on real good. Why, once on a Sunday I took him clear up to Abingdon and back, all on the one day, and he never once complained. Didn't feed him neither. Couldn't. Had no feed and had no money. . . . Lord, I hated to lose that gelding. Went down in the big fire Hallowe'en last. Trapped in the stall somehow, even after Dee opened the gates. Must've been his foot. Something. I ain't got a horse now neither. That's how come I'm out here watching you. Just come out to the hills, thinking about things, wondering why my horse is gone, why the fire happened, why Dee took off, why everything.

Breaks my train seeing you out there. Gets my mind off being alone and the kids to raise. Gets me thinking about other things, too. Time you went walking with me, down the swamps. God, we was young then, and you was a handsome goddamn woman. Wouldn't have me, though, and I sure cussed you good. Could've killed you that one night. You near about broke me, and that's the truth. Couldn't get out the bed for two, three weeks. Everyone thought I had the fever, even my Ma. Thought the horse fever'd bury me before the week was out. But that wasn't it, no sir. I was dying, all right, but it wasn't the fever. I was dying for Sadie Larkin. I think I did die there for a while.

What it was, was the cold moon and the wondering, I guess. And that kiss, Sadie—not the little peck by Blue Rock, but the one over by the stream. And you *asked* me for it, damn it. *You* come up to *me*, watching my face all the while, came right out and said, *You can kiss me, Clay. I want you to.* Well, that set off the trigger, not that it needed setting off. I was a goner the minute I seen you by the hawthorn in that long blue dress. You was quite a lady back then, so damn pretty I nearly choked on my own tongue. And you smiling on me! Been damn near dreaming about these things for fifteen years.

Never thought I'd get to kiss you back then. You was much too proper, I thought, and never looked me back in the eyes long enough. Every time I tried to tell you something, you'd flit off and talk about the cows. I should've called you on it, but what with me eighteen, I never had the what-all. Thought you'd high-tail it home and then I'd *never* get a chance.

Well, hell . . . I never got the big chance anyways, and
that's the truth. Fact is, you never really wanted me
back then. But that night by the stream, I thought
for sure I was your boy, Sade, and I was ten feet tall.

***

Sadie Larkin by the riverbed, kicking pebbles,
breathing moonlight, swishing by young Clay in blue
gingham, feeling fire in the cool night air.

Why you walking over there, Clay? she asked.

No reason, Sadie. Don't know where to put myself, I reckon.

Why don't you put yourself over here by me?

Lemme see what's shiny there by Blue Rock first.

You scared of me, Clay?

Nah. I ain't scared.

Sure now?

Yes'm.

*You know what I think? I think you are scared. Scared to
come on over here and look at me straight-eyed. And I'll look
at you, and then you take me in your nice brown arms and
hold me a minute, nice and close, but not so's I can't breathe,
just so's I can get the feel of you up and down, and then put*

your face near mine and kiss me—gentle-like at first, rubbing your big, beautiful lips against mine, back and forth a little, real slow and soft-like, and then—well—you know—getting into it a little more.

Stop that, Sadie.

C'mon, Clay.

You don't know what you're saying, Sadie.

Of course I do. You know I do.

You calling me, Sadie.

That's right—I am.

You telling me to walk on over—right now—and take you.

Just to kiss me, Clay.

You telling me to come over.

You don't want to, Clay? You don't want me?

You know I want you, Sadie. . . . That ain't it at all and you know it.

Well, then, what is it? You are scared. That's all it could be. Scared, scared—an old chicken, like Web always says. Just can't act like a man. Can't rise up.

That ain't true!

Is too!

It ain't! And if you say that again, I'm gonna have to shame you, Sadie. I won't have nobody saying I'm chicken for nothing! Even you . . . even now.

Well . . . what am I supposed to think?

Damn it, Sadie. I don't want no woman telling me to come kiss her. It ain't right.

Oh, pooh. Who cares about that?

Right's me asking you! Me telling you I want you and will you have me if I come for a kiss on my own two feet.

But you didn't ask me, Clay. What was I supposed to do, wait a month of Sundays? By that time, I'd be fixing to marry Web Taylor. You know he's been asking.

For God's sake, Sadie, what do you want with a mule-head like Web? What're you teasing with him for anyway, his pappy's money?

I ain't the type to play up for money, Clay.

Well, I ain't the type to play chicken.

OK, OK.

OK, then.

OK, then. . . . So? You coming or what?

Well—

*Clay, you making me mad. Just pretend I didn't ask first.
I'll never tell.*

You know I want to, Sadie.

I hope you do.

Want you so bad I could almost die.

*Well, I do want you . . . and I won't say it again. . . . And
the night is going by, and you are not coming to me, and pretty
soon I got to go home or Pa'll be yelling up and down the hills
to git home, and then you'll plumb lose your chance, and* then
what should I think?

There was nothing left to say, and he knew it like he
knew his name.

Now, he muttered. *I gotta do this.*

He rose up the bank and strode over the rocks,
knees weak and loose, heart beating like a scared
baby robin flying out the first time, eye-balling Sadie
as soon as he picked up on her, coming closer.

Her eyes were dancing with pleasure now she'd have
her way, and she curled up the corners of her big
berry lips, tilting her head into the moonlight just so.
Big Web Taylor always loved those curled-up lips.

Got you, Clay, she said under her breath.

But the smile went down as Clay came up, his shoulders going back, chin rising, eyes fixing her on the spot as he took himself in tow, softening Sadie Larkin right off her old high horse, though they didn't see it then, and not for a long time after.

He put his strong hands on her two arms, up by the shoulders, almost lifting her off the riverbank as his face came close.

Clay, she said, *you finally in your senses.*

Old Woods

New shoots circle like spokes
round the raw and wounded stump,
build a closing   fence around
the naked   maple flesh,
protection,   safeguards,
a bearhug cage   as the baby shoots
reach for the sky,   sweet sun tumbling in,
on jagged, mulchy hills.

Sun-Ups, Night Chills

She goes out riding, picks a horse,
          the fastest horse,
heads east when the sun comes up,
          when she catches the first rays,
when they're strong and new,
          make *her* feel new,
give her some hope to chew.

She goes to it, heads for the sun,
          rides out past the sleepy houses,
takes it all with her,
          fills the pack,
acorn nuts and water,
          extra blanket rolled tight,
throws on a shawl,
          thick one this time,
keeping out the night-mist.

She'll hold it close, that shawl,
          in despite of those wears and tears.
Night chill's the worst chill.

Turning Around Those Locomotive Blues

You can vision this, Sadie Larkin,
in your spirit of glad flight,
keeping the image strong—
in time . . . in time . . . in time.

Over the station back of town,
a black smoke-stream of burning coal,
an unclouded message—
Do I dare to move ahead? she wants to ask.
Don't you? a voice replies
      from deep in the waiting train.

Into the runaway night-lights,
she squints through the mist,
looking to the smoky engine,
top of the rollaway stairs,
open door hovering in light
      just beyond the missing last step.

Packs in hand, ticket in her belt,
she starts climbing, climbing,
looking to board for the take-off.
She pulls forward as a matter of course,
finds a sudden crescent gully
      widening as she watches.

She sees her right foot poised
and frozen over empty space,
wonders where the last step went,
where the banister turned to nowhere,
where she rustled the knot in her throat,
      where her foot should rest.

Then, like a crow on the half-wing,
she dives into the space with all her might,
scans the floor for direction,
an open lane to step in,
and gets cornered by a lamp
            blinking a message in code—

telling her, in starts and stops,
Stop that climbing! Stop where you are!
You've reached your limit, Sadie,
second to the last step.
That's all there is, see.
            You covered the distance.

She sees some red and yellow lights,
picks out the letters
as they blind her watering eyes:
S - T - O -
but she shakes her wings, she has to,
            tries marking her own time,

waiting to get her bearings,
waiting for enough beats to pass
so she can capture those bearings.
And she is thinking, there in mid-stream,
of ponies in the far south field,
            wild mare pawing the paddock floor.

Take your foot in hand, the voice says,
put it where the step should be.
Place it there directly,
where the empty step should be,
a place for a footprint,
            a solid step of corrugated steel.

Feel the empty place with your sole,
think of it built up at last,
      stairwell complete,
      landing in place,
a place to take air in,
make passage to an iron car,
hurtling through the hills
      you in the belly of a lighted snake,
      midnight crowding brown salt clouds.

Rounding the Pass 2

And she pushed her way past the berry bushes into a
narrow clearing bounded by brush and tree-trunks
slowly choking to death as the vines tightened their
lethal grip up and down the branches, growing right
around the leaf handles, themselves knowing there'd
be no leaves budding in three, four years, maybe just
a couple if the moisture's right.

Even through her boots she could feel something
like pebbles under the weeds. Damned if it wasn't a
path of some sort, a clearing, maybe a space set for
planting. She didn't see anything more'n wild weeds
around the edge, but who knows what might have
been there when the place was cleared.

She rubbed her hand along the low weeds, stopped in
time to pass the poison oak, pick up again where it
was safe and she could pull some roots might make a
brew come winter.

Some kind of restorative, she thought, *but what, I don't
know. Maybe ask Sal.*

The light was off, what could grow here? Not much
sky above, vine roots probably everywhere now,
tubers and feeding hairs filling up the spaces where
the roots could have spread, choking them out like
they weren't there first and put there to *be* something.

A wide table rock marked her place, prickly bushes
just coming together, the beginning of something—
she knew it. And it was funny how the path she took

was no path, just herself trailing through the greens, pushing her nose into the brush where she thought she could best get past, twisting and turning and backing up to find another path she knew would send her up the hill to home, two, three places, vines leaping across the narrow passes, reaching and clasping crosswise, then turning back to the other side, knowing it was their right and proper way.

And when it thickened to where it was flat in her face like a wall of fence closing her out, and she knew with a start it was the first gate, she pulled out her knife, placed the wrapping plumb into the basket at her feet, stood up, and commenced raising her hand for the first hack. She hoped one slice would do it. She never liked cutting into the wild. *Who wants to be cut?* she'd say when they mocked her for it. *Neither me nor you!*

She wrapped her left fist around the bushy leaves, coming up from the bottom, taking in as much as she could hold over her open palm and raised her right arm straight up back of her shoulders, trying for a good angle so's the blade could make the entire cut first shot. But she held the knife in the air, counted two, three, four, and felt herself loosening her grasp as she lowered the vines into place whilst her left hand dropped to her side.

It's not the way, she said, everything still as she went about her business, wrapping the knife and loading the basket onto her shoulder.

Use your head, Sadie.

She stepped toward the wall of brush on her right, roses again, bush covered with cascading branches six and seven feet long and drenched in palest pink, and it was June and the right time, and she walked right up, don't you know, so's she could smell it close, run her open hand along the petals, open flowers with her palm, murmuring *beautiful* as she moved her head near and then back, near and back, caressing the blossoms with a velvet touch, telling them it was her, Sadie Larkin, she wanted passage.

Not now, I don't know. The words formed in her mind like something from a well-spring.

She moved again, to the vines hanging like a valance about her height, then to the left, where a wall of prickers stopped her cold, freezing her in place so she backed around, taking a quiet stand, it wasn't a matter of knives or know-how now, just Sadie and the brush trying to find a way around the impasse, everyone knowing Sadie was settling now, it was probably only a matter of time before they'd work it out.

She stood her ground and waited while the dark started coming down, turning her head to see where it came from, turning back just in time to see the rose thin out, vines cut by half so's she could move slowly through, seeing her way into the forest without signs, this time knowing she was in a different place and solidly on track.

She pressed through in quiet time, looking for this and

that with calm deliberation. She walked a few steps at
a time, checked herself and all around, picking up on
the tree-sounds and crowings, birds cackling, frogs and
snakes, fox and something much larger—*but what?*—
making their moves and noises in the stillness where
Sadie Larkin was finally making way.

Seemed straight enough, her feet moving one in
front of the other, basket getting heavy as she
changed shoulders yet again, keeping on before
minds changed and the pass'd be closed.

She wasn't even paying attention overhead when the
leaves cleared and the umbrella of vines was visible,
bigger'n a mountain, coming out of some enormous
trunks, spreading out—*How could that happen?* she
asked when she saw what was right in front of her.
Where was I not to see past my nose? she asked when
there was time to recollect.

Never mind that bear, she crowed. *He'll find me if he needs
to. I'm 'a get me under that umbrella while I have the chance,
no ways waiting till the next time, and maybe rest, maybe stop
and think till I figure how to cut back out if I can cut back.*

It took many steps to reach the veil of vines,
hundreds more than she counted when she took it all
in and started walking directly there, feeling thick,
but never more clear-minded. She sensed she could
coil into something she never conjured in her wildest
dreams, a bowl, turned over to hug the earth with
pale beige ribbons, free-falling through the last
remaining branches, full up with sap, she learned that
when she cussed herself for cutting into a vine like

the one up the barn, trying to stop it from squeezing the life from her last white elm.

She was breathing like a bird when she finally covered the last few yards and stopped for a deeper breath.

I could faint away and they'd never find me. She quieted as the thought took hold, and she opened her eyes, vine-leaves right in front of her, veins a bleeding scarlet against the olive green, pulsing, it looked like, wormy, maybe liquid in their world of leaf-mold and spores, drinking up the heavy air, maybe putting out some mist of their own after changing the molds to a thickening dew.

She reached up an arm without touching, waiting to see if the leaves would turn rigid and fence her, but nothing moved and she opened her hand, fastening her notice on a small clump of vine-leaves shaped like a small fan coming forward of the other leaves and swaying some, doing a breezy dance for Sadie while the others watched, her own eyes fixed loose and graceful when it all came down to letting it be.

Damn, and she lit straight in the face of wonder, *the passage is made!*

Three Roosters Crowing Yes to the Cloud-Cover

Three roosters crowing at the absent sun—
mist so thick the world is rabbit gray.

What is this ball of life that
(hidden by the cloudbank)
inspires such raucous chorales?

The New Mare

She's a fast rider, Sadie,
willing to take the new mare
up-country, first day out.

Who does such damn fool things?

Will she never learn?
The mare might turn on her,
rear up,
throw her to the stony ground
and break her to pieces.

*What makes her think the mare's ready
just because she's ready?*

A mare wants tending,
raising, preening, feeding,
wants to know who's boss
before she takes up the saddle
and runs the field.

Who is she to chance the wild?

Riding Against All Odds

Sadie Larkin, riding rough-shod in the cold winter night.

It is Clay and Sadie early Sunday evening,
trying to fix what's passed in their glances,
cottonwoods standing their ground
as they try finding a place
in the pointy riverbed rocks.
There's a tightness in her middle parts,
tension flattening unexpected yawns.
But there's no denying the pungent spice,
mustard and sage in the snappy air,
and she is wide awake.

*Sadie Larkin goes a-riding, nine days out, no more, since
the little purple violets were dropped off, way too late
for Valentine's.*

They are walking near the north bend,
toying with flint and rocks like eggs.
She drinks his every move,
the soft humming lips and knobby hands,
thinking hard and losing time,
turning away when her mouth runs dry.

He wishes to take her home
lock, stock, barrel, and mare,
calls up hard times in the fields,
how he's done it all ten years now,
how she's done it, too. He knows.
He's been watching like a hawk.
She catches how his shoulders turn,
muscles stretching the flannel sleeves.

She can taste the fire and blood-rush,
arms locked on the dark side of the moon.

Sadie Larkin, skirts flying in the wind, long whip
in her right hand, crashing though the night, man-like,
lady-like, head up high.

They meet again just past the falls
on an old dirt road near the sedge.
She watches him bend for a walking stick,
feels her middle tighten like rope,
jumps when he catches her tearing eye,
night-wind drowning her moan.

He turns to the thousand tomorrows
there at the ranch-house,
counts off the sheep and horses,
what little trouble the kids are,
how he knows there'll be more help
come springtime, how—swallowing hard,
clearing his dusty throat—
he'll honor Sadie, adore her heart and soul,
till he just can't think no more.

She talks about keeping the farm afloat,
opening a stand near the old creek bridge,
wringing out that sodden hay
before her threads scatter.

Do it at my place, Sade!
We'll do your days at my place!
There's wildfire here—two fires, Sade,—
waiting to light our tangling flame,
waiting to lick our grate.

Sadie Larkin on the great horse, riding, riding, taking it in
as she goes, heart beating madly.

> He touches her reddening cheek,
> plants a silent kiss on her worrying lips.
> No time for wondering,
> when he's square in her face,
> singing his holding wish,
> strong hands keeping her shoulders tight.
> It is far too brisk, this rabbity pace,
> too crisp, these shallow breathings.
>
> But a chill's coming down the night air.
> Gusts bring a shower of russet leaves
> while the tree-frogs regale her.
> She can't make sense of it no-how.
> Where has it come from,
> this biting cold,
> grounding the clarifying night?

Riding it through like dense air in a close room, yet not passing by
like a coward, she's a hero, a hero, dashing through empty streets.

> Suddenly, in a lightning stroke—
> call it a message finally taken—
> it is vinegar, the choice,
> vinegar, the soft ache in her bones.
> In a whiff of pine, smoke from a distant fire,
> she cannot go the distance,
> hasn't the muscle or arrogance for it,
> not with the fragrant breeze blowing wild
> in the black and white air.

But this one fire that stokes the burning night
she'll see to its destined end—
quiet her aching head,
soften his stone sorrow with honey and soup
and porridge and coffee and cream.

And he'll take heart from the feel of her
this one night, find footing
in the wild winds and lightning thunder
coming around the bluff.
She'll have Clay gallop with her, sure,
just this once while the winds build,
carving their tracks across the hay-fields,
him singing his wondrous man-song
while she is singing hers,
moonrise low and red against the tree-tops,
Sadie flying high and wide.

*She is riding it out against all odds, Valentine flowers in back
of her gray-green eyes, jubilation in her voice as she shouts
in the cold night air, her riding song.*

> Put on your boots, Sadie Larkin,
> put on your scarlet cape,
> your great leather belt.
> You erred, old girl, you did right.
> Go post your horse
> and come on in.
> Tea-water's finally hot.

Winter Woodcut

Heaven's biggest dipper penetrates
the tree bones,
keeps her company
up the silent path.

A little dog whines,
scratches a wooden door
till it opens
to her scampering bark
and a sudden shaft of light.

Then it's starlit darkness.

A twig snaps in the brush,
an old leaf falls.

Two orange beams
in the face of a wildcat
mark the flattened earth
and she breathes again,
taking in the cold air,
wagging her head,
nodding how the road winds true.

Fanning the Forest Flame

What are your fancies?
What are your daydreams?
I'll cook, she whispers, voice condensed,
eyes on a crystal pool.

I'll be wild and free
    in the chill November dusk,
    music welling as the wind whips,
    so wild you'll never know me
    on the jagged rocks and boulders.

The volcano born in the mountain's bowel
    will never sleep, lava pushing
    to the open air where it spills out
    in an explosion of darks and lights,
    reds purples browns and blacks,
    heat cracking gray-white ash
    in maddening patterns like veins,
    like underground rivers carving a cave,
    eating it out in complicated lines
    so brilliant in their frenzy,
    so hungry in their grip on the rock.

I will lose me in the heat of that eruption.
    It will be—again, and then again some—
    the endless forming and re-forming
    of the first, last, and greatest expression
    of Sadie Larkin, volcano goddess,
    rising from underground flames.

You can find me there,
    staring into the well at my feet,
    down to the deepest springs

where molten threads
upsurge and ring me round
on the highest cliffs,
in the coolest valley cleft,
tying knots around the beating heart
of Sadie Larkin, wild one.

I will meet you and stake my claim,
bare feet in red ash,
hands and arms in the verdant air
of an autumn afternoon,
tossing a fury of thunder
between the heat and the cold,
one raw no and a yes.

Meet me.
I have gifts I burn to bestow
with charged fingers,
words, taste, delicate touch on fur,
feasts and trials,
songs in echoing voice.

There will be flowers and fragrance of spring,
flaming forsythia, lilac,
daffodils yellow and white,
full moons and patchy charcoal clouds,
silver birds crossing the land,
aiming with rank precision
at the mountain's open mouth.

That's where you'll find Sadie Larkin, boys,
riding her hot-blooded mare,
clip-clopping over the burning coals,
the embrace of earth and sky

over curved wet flanks,
fingertips on alert,
commands resting on the tips of tongues,
secrets surfacing like hidden trinkets
in the darkening heat,
embers grinning like cats
on the great corner stove.

Then let the music fly, she moves along,
eyes flashing emerald and pewter,
liquid pulling in,
copper buttons and silver strings
singing wayward, unheard songs,
and—let the dance begin.

Printed in the United States
146248LV00003B/49/A